HOW TO THRIVE IN A RELATIONSHIP WITH A NARCISSISTIC PARTNER

TABLE OF CONTENTS

Introduction

In the intricate dance of human relationships, encountering a partner with Narcissistic Personality Disorder (NPD) introduces a unique set of challenges. This introduction serves as a compass, guiding you through the labyrinth of narcissism, shedding light on its manifestations, and offering insights into the importance of comprehending and addressing these challenges.

The Narcissistic Landscape:

Narcissistic Personality Disorder, a complex mental health condition, is characterized by a pervasive pattern of grandiosity, a constant need for admiration, and a lack of empathy. As we embark on this exploration, it is crucial to grasp the intricacies of NPD, recognizing that individuals with this disorder often struggle with maintaining healthy and reciprocal relationships.

Narcissism isn't merely an inflated sense of self; it's a spectrum of behaviors that can profoundly impact the dynamics of an intimate partnership. From a relentless desire for validation to a tendency to exploit others emotionally, the traits of NPD shape the emotional landscape of those involved.

Understanding the Layers:

To navigate the challenges posed by a narcissistic partner, one must first unravel the layers of this intricate personality disorder. We delve into the depths of narcissistic behavior, examining the facade of self-importance that conceals the fragility beneath. Understanding the root causes and the emotional mechanisms at play is the first step toward developing effective coping strategies.

Behind the Mask:

Narcissistic individuals often present a polished exterior that conceals a fragile self-esteem. We explore the emotional vulnerabilities that drive narcissistic behavior, shedding light on the paradox of grandiosity masking deep-seated insecurities. This understanding serves as a foundation for compassion and informed decision-making within the relationship.

The Narcissistic Puzzle:

Narcissistic Personality Disorder isn't just a psychological term; it's a way of navigating the world that affects how individuals connect with others. Imagine a puzzle where each piece represents a trait – an unrelenting need for admiration, an inflated sense of self-importance, and a lack of empathy. To navigate this puzzle, we need to understand each piece and how they fit together.

Peeling Back the Layers:

Think of a narcissistic partner as an onion with many layers. Beyond the polished exterior lies a delicate inner core, often masked by grandiosity. It's not just about an obsession with oneself; it's about the intricate dance between a craving for validation and an underlying fragility. Understanding these layers is the first step in developing strategies to cope within the relationship.

Unmasking the Vulnerability:

Narcissistic individuals often wear a mask of invincibility, but underneath, there's vulnerability. Peel back the layers, and you'll discover the paradox – an apparent self-assurance concealing deep-seated insecurities. Recognizing and empathizing with these vulnerabilities is key to navigating the emotional terrain of a relationship with a narcissistic partner.

Narcissism in Relationships:

As we navigate the realm of narcissism, we confront its impact on interpersonal dynamics. The narcissistic partner's difficulty in empathizing and connecting emotionally can lead to a series of challenges for their counterpart. Unpacking the emotional toll and recognizing the signs of emotional manipulation and abuse is crucial for those traversing this intricate terrain.

Understanding and Addressing the Challenges in a Relationship with a Narcissistic Partner

Navigating a relationship with a narcissistic partner is akin to embarking on a complex journey where emotional landscapes shift unpredictably. In this section, we'll delve into the profound importance of not only understanding but actively addressing the challenges that arise when love intertwines with narcissism.

The Ripple Effect of Narcissism:

Imagine your relationship as a pond, its surface reflecting the harmony you seek. Now, introduce the stone of narcissism – the ripples of self-centered behaviors, constant need for validation, and emotional detachment. Understanding these ripples is crucial, for they impact not only your emotional well-being but also the overall dynamic of your connection.

Preserving Your Emotional Sanctuary:

Your emotional well-being is at the heart of any relationship. A narcissistic partner's behaviors can create turbulence in this emotional sanctuary, leaving you feeling drained and questioning your own worth. By understanding the impact of these behaviors, you gain the tools to protect your emotional space, preserving a sense of self amidst the storm.

Breaking the Silence:

One common challenge in relationships with narcissistic partners is the silence that often accompanies emotional struggles. Whether it's due to fear of repercussions or a sense of futility, addressing issues becomes a daunting task. Here, we emphasize the importance of breaking this silence – voicing concerns, expressing needs, and fostering open communication as a catalyst for positive change.

The Empathy Conundrum:

Empathy, the glue that binds relationships, can be notably absent in the dynamics of a narcissistic partnership. Understanding the absence of empathy is not just about identifying a problem but a key step towards forging strategies to cope. It involves recognizing that the challenge lies in the very nature of the disorder, fostering a sense of empathy for both your partner and, importantly, for yourself.

Recognizing Emotional Manipulation:

Navigating a relationship with a narcissistic partner often involves navigating through a maze of emotional manipulation. Recognizing the signs is pivotal – from subtle guilt-tripping to more overt attempts at control. By understanding these manipulative tactics, you equip yourself with the discernment needed to maintain a sense of agency and autonomy within the relationship.

The Art of Setting Boundaries:

Amidst the challenges, setting and maintaining boundaries becomes an art form. This involves not only recognizing the need for boundaries but also communicating them effectively. By understanding that boundaries are not walls but expressions of self-respect, you lay the foundation for a healthier dynamic, where your emotional needs are acknowledged and respected.

Preserving Your Identity:

One of the profound impacts of a relationship with a narcissistic partner is the potential erosion of one's identity. It's easy to become entangled in the web of their needs and demands, losing sight of your own aspirations. Recognizing the importance of preserving your identity becomes a cornerstone of addressing challenges – a reminder that you are more than a supporting character in your own narrative.

Seeking Professional Guidance:

Understanding the depth of challenges in a relationship with a narcissistic partner often leads to a crossroads where seeking professional guidance becomes paramount. Whether through individual therapy or couples counseling, the insight and tools provided by a professional can be transformative. Recognizing that seeking help is not a sign of weakness but a courageous step towards healing is a pivotal realization.

Cultivating Resilience:

As we explore the importance of understanding and addressing challenges, we underscore the significance of cultivating resilience. It's an acknowledgment that while the journey may be arduous, it's within your power to not just endure but to grow stronger through the process. Understanding challenges becomes a catalyst for personal growth and empowerment.

In the forthcoming chapters, we'll delve deeper into practical strategies and insights to navigate these challenges effectively. Remember, you are not alone on this journey. By understanding the intricacies of your relationship and actively addressing the challenges, you lay the groundwork for a path towards resilience, empowerment, and ultimately, a healthier connection.

Chapter 1: Understanding Narcissistic Behavior

Welcome to the first chapter of our guide, where we'll dive into the fascinating realm of narcissistic behavior. Understanding the characteristics and traits of Narcissistic Personality Disorder (NPD) is like deciphering a unique language that shapes the dynamics of relationships. So, grab a metaphorical magnifying glass, and let's explore this captivating landscape.

The Narcissistic Spectrum:

Narcissistic Personality Disorder is not a one-size-fits-all condition; it exists on a spectrum, manifesting in various degrees and combinations of traits. At one end, you might encounter someone with a pronounced need for admiration and an inflated sense of self-importance. On the other, more severe end, there could be a pervasive pattern of exploiting others for personal gain with a complete lack of empathy.

Traits of NPD:

At the core of narcissistic behavior are distinctive traits that collectively paint the portrait of NPD.

Grandiosity: Narcissists often harbor an exaggerated sense of their own abilities and achievements. They may overstate their accomplishments and expect others to recognize their superiority.

Need for Admiration: Seeking constant admiration is a hallmark trait. Narcissists crave validation, requiring others to acknowledge and praise their perceived brilliance and achievements regularly.

Lack of Empathy: Empathy, the ability to understand and share the feelings of others, is notably absent in those with NPD. This absence can profoundly impact how they relate to and connect with others.

Sense of Entitlement: Narcissists often believe they are entitled to special treatment. This entitlement may manifest in expecting others to fulfill their needs without reciprocation.

Exploitative Behavior: In pursuit of their desires, narcissists may exploit others. This can range from taking advantage of someone emotionally to manipulating situations for personal gain.

Envy and Belief Others are Envious: Narcissists may harbor envy towards others while simultaneously believing that others are envious of them. This duality contributes to a constant comparison and competition dynamic.

Arrogance: An air of arrogance often accompanies narcissistic individuals. They may display a condescending attitude, belittling others to reinforce their own perceived superiority.

Understanding these traits offers a roadmap to deciphering narcissistic behavior. It's important to note that individuals with NPD may display a combination of these traits, and the intensity can vary.

The Narcissistic Mask:

Imagine a mask that a narcissist wears - a facade that conceals vulnerabilities and insecurities. Behind this mask lies a complex interplay of self-assurance and fragility. Understanding the art of this disguise is crucial; it's not just about recognizing arrogance but peeling back the layers to reveal the emotional intricacies beneath.

The Fragile Core:

Beneath the grandiose exterior, many narcissists harbor a fragile core. Understanding this vulnerability is a key element in navigating relationships with narcissistic individuals. It's about acknowledging that, despite the outward confidence, there exists a delicate balance between the need for validation and a fear of rejection.

Coping Mechanisms:

To truly understand narcissistic behavior, we must explore the coping mechanisms employed by individuals with NPD. These mechanisms often serve as shields, protecting the fragile ego while influencing how they interact within relationships. From projection, where they attribute their own shortcomings to others, to gaslighting, a tactic designed to make someone doubt their own perceptions, these mechanisms shape the intricate dance of narcissistic behavior.

Understanding Narcissistic Behavior

Now that we've familiarized ourselves with the traits of Narcissistic Personality Disorder (NPD), let's shine a light on how these characteristics weave into the intricate tapestry of relationships. Understanding how narcissistic behavior manifests in these personal connections is like deciphering a unique dance, where the rhythm can be both enchanting and challenging.

The Charm Offensive:

At the onset of a relationship with a narcissistic partner, you might encounter what is often referred to as the "charm offensive." Picture a charismatic individual, exuding confidence and charisma, drawing you into their orbit with compliments and a seemingly genuine interest in your life. This initial phase is characterized by an overwhelming display of affection and attention, creating a captivating illusion.

Love-Bombing:

A prominent manifestation of narcissistic behavior in relationships is the phenomenon known as "love-bombing." This is an intense and rapid display of affection, where the narcissistic partner showers you with love, admiration, and gifts. While this may initially feel like a fairytale romance, it's essential to recognize it as a potential precursor to the more challenging aspects of narcissistic behavior.

Control and Manipulation:

As the relationship progresses, narcissists may subtly introduce control and manipulation into the dynamics. This can range from making decisions unilaterally to employing guilt-trips as a means of swaying your choices. The goal is to establish dominance and maintain a sense of superiority within the relationship.

The Emotional Rollercoaster:

Navigating a relationship with a narcissistic partner often feels like riding an emotional rollercoaster. The highs of adoration and affirmation are juxtaposed with sudden lows, where criticism, blame, and emotional distance become prevalent. This erratic pattern can leave you feeling bewildered and emotionally drained.

Gaslighting:

One of the more insidious manifestations of narcissistic behavior is gaslighting. This manipulative tactic involves distorting or denying reality to make you doubt your own perceptions. It's a form of psychological control that can leave you questioning your sanity and the validity of your feelings.

Projecting Insecurities:

Narcissists often project their own insecurities onto their partners. If they harbor feelings of inadequacy, they may criticize you for perceived flaws. Understanding that these critiques often stem from their own internal struggles can provide a measure of clarity amidst the emotional turmoil.

Isolating Tactics:

In an effort to maintain control, narcissists may employ isolating tactics. This could involve subtly distancing you from friends and family or insisting on controlling your social interactions. Recognizing these attempts to limit your support network is crucial for maintaining a sense of independence.

Emotional Withdrawal:

When their need for admiration is not met or if they perceive a threat to their perceived superiority, narcissists may emotionally withdraw. This withdrawal can leave you feeling abandoned and questioning your worth, reinforcing the power dynamic in the relationship.

Triangulation:

Narcissistic partners may engage in triangulation, introducing a third party into the dynamic to create jealousy or competition. This tactic not only reinforces their need for admiration but also destabilizes your sense of security within the relationship.

The Devaluation Phase:

After the initial idealization phase, a narcissistic partner may enter the devaluation phase, where the charming facade crumbles, and criticisms and insults become more pronounced. This phase can be emotionally tumultuous, as the partner's perception of you shifts from idealized to devalued.

Hoovering:

As a means of maintaining control, narcissistic partners may employ hoovering, a tactic named after the vacuum cleaner, as it involves attempting to suck you back into the relationship. This can manifest as sudden displays of affection, promises of change, or apologies after a period of emotional distance or abuse.

Understanding how narcissistic behavior manifests in relationships is crucial for developing strategies to navigate these challenges. In the subsequent chapters, we'll explore coping mechanisms, communication strategies, and the path to empowerment within the context of a relationship with a narcissistic partner. Stay tuned for insights that will empower you to thrive amidst the complexities of narcissism.

Chapter 2: Impact on the Partner: Navigating the Emotional Landscape

In the intricate dance of a relationship with a narcissistic partner, the non-narcissistic individual often finds themselves navigating a challenging emotional terrain. In this chapter, we'll explore the profound impact of living with a narcissist on the partner's emotional and psychological well-being, shedding light on the complexities that unfold beneath the surface.

Emotional Rollercoaster:

A relationship with a narcissistic partner often feels like an unpredictable emotional rollercoaster. The partner experiences highs of adoration and affection, only to be plunged into lows of criticism, blame, and emotional distance. This erratic pattern can leave the non-narcissistic partner feeling bewildered, anxious, and emotionally drained.

Self-Esteem Erosion:

One of the insidious effects of living with a narcissistic partner is the erosion of self-esteem. The constant need for validation and the ever-shifting dynamics can leave the non-narcissistic individual questioning their worth. The partner may find themselves contending with feelings of inadequacy and self-doubt as they attempt to navigate the turbulent emotional landscape.

Guilt and Blame:

Narcissistic partners are adept at deflecting blame and instilling guilt. The non-narcissistic partner may find themselves shouldering the blame for relationship issues, even when they are not at fault. This manipulation can contribute to a pervasive sense of guilt, further impacting the emotional well-being of the partner.

Isolation and Alienation:

Narcissistic partners may employ tactics that isolate the non-narcissistic individual from their support network. Whether subtly undermining relationships with friends and family or insisting on controlling social interactions, this isolation can lead to feelings of alienation. The partner may find themselves increasingly isolated, lacking the emotional support needed to navigate the challenges within the relationship.

Walking on Eggshells:

Living with a narcissistic partner often involves a constant tiptoeing around their moods and reactions. The non-narcissistic individual may develop a heightened sense of vigilance, always wary of triggering negative responses. This hypervigilance can contribute to chronic stress and anxiety, as the partner endeavors to maintain a semblance of peace within the relationship.

Emotional Withdrawal and Desensitization:

In response to the emotional tumult within the relationship, the non-narcissistic partner may experience emotional withdrawal as a coping mechanism. This withdrawal can lead to a desensitization to their own emotions, as they learn to suppress or downplay their feelings to avoid conflict. Over time, this emotional numbing can impact the partner's ability to connect authentically with their own emotions.

Loss of Identity:

The narcissistic dynamic often places the non-narcissistic partner in a supporting role, where their own needs and aspirations take a backseat. This can lead to a profound loss of identity as the partner becomes enmeshed in the narcissist's world. Recognizing and addressing this loss of self is crucial for reclaiming autonomy and personal fulfillment.

Chronic Stress and Anxiety:

The constant unpredictability and emotional turbulence within a relationship with a narcissistic partner contribute to chronic stress and anxiety. The non-narcissistic partner may find themselves in a perpetual state of alertness, anticipating the next emotional upheaval. This chronic stress can manifest physically, affecting overall well-being.

Coping Mechanisms and Resilience:

Despite the challenges, non-narcissistic partners often develop coping mechanisms and resilience. Whether through seeking therapy, establishing boundaries, or cultivating a support network, these strategies can empower the partner to navigate the emotional impact of the relationship. Recognizing the importance of self-care and prioritizing mental health becomes a crucial step towards building resilience in the face of adversity.

In the subsequent sections, we'll delve into recognizing signs of emotional manipulation and abuse, offering insights and strategies for the non-narcissistic partner to navigate the complexities of their emotional landscape. Stay tuned for empowering revelations that will guide you towards resilience and self-discovery amidst the challenges of a relationship with a narcissistic partner.

Recognizing Signs of Emotional Manipulation and Abuse

Navigating a relationship with a narcissistic partner often involves deciphering subtle and insidious signs of emotional manipulation and abuse. In this chapter, we'll delve into these signs, empowering non-narcissistic partners to recognize and understand the emotional dynamics at play within their relationship.

Gaslighting:

Gaslighting is a pervasive form of emotional manipulation that leaves the non-narcissistic partner questioning their own reality. The narcissistic partner distorts or denies facts, making the partner doubt their perceptions and memories. Recognizing gaslighting involves acknowledging when your experiences are being dismissed or invalidated, and trusting your instincts when something feels amiss.

Projection:

Narcissistic individuals often project their own insecurities onto their partners. If the narcissist feels inadequate, they may criticize the non-narcissistic partner for perceived flaws. Recognizing projection involves understanding that the criticisms may reflect more about the narcissist's internal struggles than the partner's actual shortcomings.

Idealization and Devaluation:

The cycle of idealization and devaluation is a hallmark of narcissistic relationships. Initially, the non-narcissistic partner is idealized, showered with affection and admiration. However, this idealization is often followed by a devaluation phase, where criticisms and insults become more pronounced. Recognizing this pattern involves being attuned to abrupt shifts in the partner's behavior and understanding that the devaluation is not a reflection of the partner's worth.

Love-Bombing and Hoovering:

Love-bombing, an intense display of affection and admiration, is often employed by narcissists to draw their partners in. However, this can be followed by hoovering, where the narcissistic partner attempts to pull the partner back into the relationship after a period of emotional distance or abuse. Recognizing these tactics involves understanding the cyclical nature of affection and withdrawal, and being cautious of sudden displays of love following periods of mistreatment.

Manipulative Guilt-Tripping:

Narcissistic partners are adept at using guilt as a tool for manipulation. They may employ guilt-tripping tactics to make the non-narcissistic partner feel responsible for the narcissist's emotional state or the overall state of the relationship. Recognizing manipulative guilt-tripping involves being aware of shifts in emotional responsibility and setting boundaries to protect against undue guilt.

Isolation Strategies:

Narcissistic individuals may employ subtle tactics to isolate their partners from friends and family. This could involve undermining existing relationships or insisting on controlling social interactions. Recognizing isolation strategies involves staying vigilant to changes in the partner's social connections and maintaining open communication about these dynamics.

Control Over Finances and Decision-Making:

Exerting control over finances and decision-making is a form of power manipulation within a narcissistic relationship. The non-narcissistic partner may find themselves stripped of financial autonomy or excluded from significant decisions. Recognizing these control tactics involves acknowledging disparities in decision-making power and financial control.

Emotional Withdrawal as Punishment:

Narcissistic partners may use emotional withdrawal as a form of punishment. If their need for admiration is not met or if they perceive a threat to their superiority, they may emotionally withdraw. Recognizing emotional withdrawal involves understanding that the partner's emotional distance may be a tactic to regain control and provoke a reaction.

Pattern of Criticism and Negativity:

Consistent criticism and negativity from the narcissistic partner contribute to emotional abuse. Recognizing this pattern involves being attuned to constant belittling, derogatory comments, or a pervasive sense of dissatisfaction expressed by the narcissistic partner.

Physical and Verbal Aggression:

In extreme cases, emotional abuse may escalate to physical or verbal aggression. Recognizing signs of physical or verbal abuse involves understanding that any form of physical harm or threatening language is unacceptable and should be addressed promptly.

Building Resilience and Seeking Support:

Recognizing these signs is a crucial step towards breaking free from the cycle of emotional manipulation and abuse. Non-narcissistic partners are encouraged to build resilience through self-care practices, establishing boundaries, and seeking support from friends, family, or professionals.

In the following chapters, we'll explore strategies for setting boundaries, effective communication, and the path to empowerment within the context of a relationship with a narcissistic partner. Stay tuned for insights that will guide you towards reclaiming control over your emotional well-being and navigating the complexities of narcissism with resilience and strength.

Chapter 3: Setting Boundaries: Navigating the Path to Empowerment

In the intricate dance of a relationship with a narcissistic partner, setting and maintaining clear boundaries becomes a powerful tool for the non-narcissistic individual. In this chapter, we'll explore the profound importance of establishing boundaries and delve into why they are crucial in reclaiming control over one's emotional well-being.

The Foundation of Self-Respect:

Imagine boundaries as the sturdy fence that defines and protects your emotional landscape. They are the non-negotiable limits that safeguard your well-being, signaling to yourself and others that your feelings, needs, and identity are worthy of respect. Establishing boundaries is, at its core, an act of self-respect.

Protection Against Emotional Manipulation:

Narcissistic partners, with their inclination towards emotional manipulation, often test the limits of their non-narcissistic counterparts. Clear boundaries act as a shield, offering protection against manipulation and preserving the partner's autonomy. When boundaries are communicated and enforced, it becomes more challenging for the narcissistic partner to breach emotional limits.

Preservation of Emotional Energy:

Navigating a relationship with a narcissistic partner can be emotionally exhausting. Clear boundaries serve as a filter, allowing positive and supportive energy to flow while preventing the draining effects of emotional manipulation. By defining what is acceptable and what is not, non-narcissistic individuals can preserve their emotional energy for self-care and personal growth.

Fostering Healthy Communication:

Boundaries are not walls; they are bridges to healthier communication. Clearly defined limits create an environment where open and honest communication can thrive. By expressing needs, concerns, and expectations, non-narcissistic partners lay the groundwork for a more transparent and authentic connection within the relationship.

Autonomy in Decision-Making:

Narcissistic partners may attempt to exert control over various aspects of the non-narcissistic individual's life, from major decisions to daily choices. Establishing boundaries reinforces autonomy in decision-making. It's a declaration that certain aspects of one's life are not open to manipulation or dominance, fostering a sense of independence and self-determination.

Preserving Individual Identity:

In the dynamic of a narcissistic relationship, it's easy for the non-narcissistic partner to lose sight of their individual identity. Boundaries act as a safeguard, ensuring that personal values, goals, and aspirations remain intact. They are a reminder that, even within the intricacies of a relationship, each individual retains a unique identity deserving of recognition and respect.

Reduction of Stress and Anxiety:

The constant uncertainty and emotional volatility within a relationship with a narcissistic partner contribute to heightened stress and anxiety. Clear boundaries function as stabilizers, reducing the unpredictability and providing a sense of control. When individuals feel empowered to set and enforce boundaries, it contributes to a healthier emotional state.

Steps to Establishing Effective Boundaries:

Self-Reflection: Begin by reflecting on your own needs, values, and limits. What are the behaviors or situations that make you uncomfortable or compromise your well-being? Understanding yourself is the first step towards articulating clear boundaries.

Identify Key Areas: Pinpoint specific areas in your life where boundaries are crucial. This could include personal space, decision-making processes, time commitments, or emotional exchanges. By targeting key areas, you can create a focused and effective boundary-setting strategy.

Communication is Key: Clearly communicate your boundaries with your partner. Use "I" statements to express your feelings and needs, focusing on how certain behaviors impact you emotionally. Be assertive yet respectful in your communication.

Consistent Enforcement: Boundaries are only effective when consistently enforced. Be firm in upholding your limits, even in the face of resistance or manipulation. Consistency reinforces the message that your boundaries are non-negotiable.

Seek Support: Share your boundaries with a trusted support network, whether friends, family, or a therapist. Having allies who understand and respect your limits provides additional reinforcement and encouragement.

Self-Care Practices: Setting and maintaining boundaries is an ongoing process that requires self-care. Prioritize activities that rejuvenate your emotional and mental well-being. Whether it's engaging in hobbies, practicing mindfulness, or seeking professional support, self-care fortifies your ability to navigate the challenges of a narcissistic relationship.

Next, we'll explore strategies for communicating boundaries effectively, offering practical insights and tools for non-narcissistic partners to assert their needs within the context of the relationship. Stay tuned for empowering revelations that will guide you towards a path of self-empowerment and resilience.

Strategies for Communicating Boundaries Effectively

Effectively communicating boundaries within a relationship with a narcissistic partner requires a thoughtful and strategic approach. In this section, we'll delve into detailed strategies that empower non-narcissistic individuals to articulate and uphold their boundaries with clarity and confidence.

1. Self-Awareness and Clarity:

Before engaging in boundary-setting conversations, it's essential to be clear about your own needs, values, and limits. Take time for self-reflection to identify specific areas where you feel boundaries are necessary. This self-awareness forms the foundation for articulate communication and provides a roadmap for expressing your needs.

2. Use "I" Statements:

When communicating boundaries, frame your statements using "I" language. Instead of saying, "You always do this," say, "I feel uncomfortable when this happens." This shifts the focus from blaming the partner to expressing your own feelings and needs. "I" statements promote open communication and reduce defensiveness.

3. Be Specific and Concrete:

Vague or ambiguous boundaries can lead to misunderstandings. Clearly define your boundaries with specific and concrete language. For example, instead of saying, "I need more space," specify, "I need at least an hour of alone time every evening to recharge."

4. Choose the Right Time and Setting:

Timing and setting play a crucial role in effective communication. Choose a time when both you and your partner can engage in a conversation without distractions or time constraints. Creating a calm and conducive environment fosters a more open and productive dialogue.

5. Express Your Feelings:

Connect your boundaries to your emotions. Express how specific behaviors make you feel and why certain limits are important to your emotional well-being. For example, say, "When certain comments are made, I feel hurt and disrespected. It's important for me to establish a boundary around such remarks."

6. Use Positive Reinforcement:

Reinforce your partner's positive behaviors when they respect your boundaries. Positive reinforcement encourages a supportive environment and reinforces the importance of mutual respect. Acknowledge and appreciate moments when your partner respects the established boundaries.

7. Be Firm and Consistent:

Consistency is key to effective boundary-setting. Clearly communicate your limits and be firm in upholding them. Avoid wavering or compromising on boundaries without careful consideration. Consistency reinforces the message that your boundaries are non-negotiable.

8. Set Consequences:

Clearly articulate consequences for crossing established boundaries. These consequences should be reasonable and proportionate to the boundary violation. For example, "If this behavior continues, I will need to take some time apart to reflect on our relationship."

9. Use Non-Defensive Language:

Maintain a non-defensive tone when communicating boundaries. Avoid accusatory language or blame, as it can escalate tension. Stay focused on expressing your needs without attacking the character of your partner. This promotes a more constructive and less confrontational conversation.

10. Utilize Written Communication:

In situations where verbal communication may be challenging, consider using written communication. This could be through a letter, email, or even a shared document. Written communication allows you to articulate your thoughts with precision and provides your partner with time to process the information.

11. Seek Professional Support:

In some cases, seeking the guidance of a therapist or counselor can facilitate the boundary-setting process. A neutral third party can provide insights, mediate discussions, and offer tools for effective communication within the context of a narcissistic relationship.

12. Practice Active Listening:

Effective communication is a two-way street. Practice active listening to understand your partner's perspective. While asserting your boundaries, create space for your partner to express their thoughts and feelings. This can foster a more collaborative approach to establishing mutually respectful boundaries.

13. Use Positive Language:

Frame your boundaries in positive language whenever possible. Instead of saying, "Don't do this," say, "I would appreciate it if you could do this instead." Positive language helps create a more cooperative and less confrontational atmosphere.

14. Reinforce Boundaries through Actions:

Words alone may not be sufficient to communicate boundaries effectively. Reinforce your verbal communication with consistent actions that align with your established limits. This strengthens the message and reinforces the importance of respecting boundaries.

15. Know When to Walk Away:

In certain situations, it may be necessary to recognize when a boundary is consistently violated with no signs of respect. Knowing when to walk away from a conversation or even the relationship is an essential aspect of self-preservation.

Empowering through Effective Communication

Effectively communicating boundaries within a relationship with a narcissistic partner is a multifaceted skill that involves self-awareness, clarity, and strategic engagement. By employing these detailed strategies, non-narcissistic individuals can navigate the complexities of boundary-setting with confidence, fostering an environment of mutual respect and self-empowerment. In the upcoming sections, we'll further explore strategies for navigating communication challenges and empowering individuals within the context of a relationship with a narcissistic partner. Stay tuned for insights that will guide you towards resilience and strength amidst the intricacies of narcissism.

Chapter 4: Self-Care and Well-being: Nurturing Your Mental and Emotional Health

In the intricate dance of a relationship with a narcissistic partner, prioritizing mental and emotional health through self-care becomes a beacon of strength and resilience. This chapter explores the profound importance of self-care, provides real-life examples of nurturing well-being, and incorporates factual information from reputable sources to underscore the proven benefits.

Understanding the Impact of Narcissistic Relationships on Mental Health:

Before delving into the strategies of self-care, it's crucial to acknowledge the impact of narcissistic relationships on mental health. The emotional rollercoaster, manipulation, and constant tension within such relationships can contribute to stress, anxiety, depression, and even symptoms of trauma. Recognizing these potential effects underscores the importance of prioritizing mental and emotional well-being.

Factual Insight:

According to the American Psychological Association (APA), individuals in relationships with narcissists may experience heightened levels of stress due to the unpredictability, emotional manipulation, and frequent power struggles within such dynamics. Chronic stress can have detrimental effects on both mental and physical health, making self-care practices essential for mitigating these impacts.

Real-Life Examples of Self-Care Practices:

Establishing Healthy Boundaries:

Real-life Example: Sarah, navigating a relationship with a narcissistic partner, began setting clear boundaries to protect her mental and emotional well-being. She communicated limits on negative behaviors, ensured personal space, and enforced consequences for boundary violations.

Engaging in Mindfulness and Meditation:

Real-life Example: Mark, facing constant emotional turbulence in his relationship, incorporated mindfulness and meditation into his daily routine. Taking a few minutes each day to focus on the present moment helped him reduce stress and maintain emotional balance.

Building a Support System:

Real-life Example: Olivia, recognizing the need for external support, cultivated a strong network of friends, family, and a therapist. Having a support system provided her with outlets for expression, validation, and guidance.

Pursuing Hobbies and Passion Projects:

Real-life Example: James, amidst the challenges of his relationship, immersed himself in a long-neglected hobby. Painting became a therapeutic outlet, offering him a creative space to express emotions and temporarily escape the stressors of his relationship.

Prioritizing Physical Health:

Real-life Example: Emma, aware of the mind-body connection, prioritized her physical health. Regular exercise, a balanced diet, and sufficient sleep became integral components of her self-care routine, enhancing her overall well-being.

Factual Insight:

Research published in the Journal of Clinical Psychology suggests that self-care practices, including mindfulness, building social connections, and engaging in enjoyable activities, can contribute to improved mental health outcomes. These practices are associated with reduced symptoms of anxiety and depression, enhancing overall psychological well-being.

Developing Self-Care Routines and Practices:

Mindfulness and Meditation:

Incorporate mindfulness exercises, such as deep breathing or guided meditation, into your daily routine. Apps like Headspace or Calm can provide accessible guided sessions.

Establishing Daily Rituals:

Create daily rituals that bring joy and relaxation. This could be a morning walk, a soothing cup of tea, or a few moments of reflection before bed.

Engaging in Physical Activity:

Prioritize regular exercise, whether it's a workout routine, yoga, or a simple walk. Physical activity is proven to release endorphins, promoting a positive mood.

Building a Support Network:

Cultivate connections with friends, family, or support groups. Having a reliable support network provides outlets for expression and understanding.

Setting Technology Boundaries:

Establish boundaries for technology use, especially in the context of a narcissistic relationship. Consider designated times for disconnecting to create mental space.

Journaling and Reflection:

Engage in journaling to express thoughts and emotions. Regular reflection can provide insights into your feelings and contribute to a sense of clarity.

Professional Therapy:

Seek therapy with a mental health professional experienced in narcissistic relationships. Therapy offers a safe space for exploration, validation, and coping strategies.

Mindful Nutrition:

Pay attention to your nutritional intake. A balanced diet can impact mood and energy levels. Consider consulting with a nutritionist for personalized guidance.

Creative Outlets:

Explore creative outlets that bring joy and expression. Whether it's art, music, or writing, engaging in creative activities fosters emotional release.

Quality Sleep:

Prioritize sufficient and quality sleep. Sleep plays a crucial role in mental and emotional well-being, affecting mood, cognition, and stress resilience.

Factual Insight:

According to the World Health Organization (WHO), self-care is recognized as a vital aspect of maintaining mental health and well-being. Adopting self-care practices contributes to stress reduction, improved emotional resilience, and enhanced overall quality of life.

In the forthcoming sections, we'll delve into additional strategies for navigating communication challenges and empowering individuals within the context of a relationship with a narcissistic partner. Stay tuned for insights that will guide you towards resilience and strength amidst the intricacies of narcissism.

Nurturing Your Inner Strength

Embarking on the journey of self-care is an empowering step towards reclaiming mental and emotional well-being within the complexities of a relationship with a narcissistic partner. In this section, we'll also explore practical examples of self-care routines and practices, and share a real-life story illustrating the positive impact of such intentional self-nurturing.

Examples of Self-Care Routines:

Morning Mindfulness Routine:

Begin your day with a few minutes of mindfulness. Engage in deep breathing exercises or a short meditation to set a positive tone for the day.

Daily Gratitude Practice:

Dedicate a moment each day to reflect on things you are grateful for. Whether it's a supportive friend, a small accomplishment, or a moment of peace, expressing gratitude can shift your focus to positive aspects of your life.

Tech-Free Evenings:

Establish boundaries for technology use in the evenings. Designate a specific time to disconnect from screens and engage in activities that promote relaxation, such as reading, journaling, or enjoying a quiet evening walk.

Weekly Nature Connection:

Carve out time each week for a nature-based activity. This could be a hike, a walk in the park, or simply sitting in a garden. Nature has proven therapeutic effects on mental well-being.

Creative Expression Breaks:

Integrate short breaks for creative expression throughout your day. Whether it's doodling, writing a poem, or playing a musical instrument, these moments of creativity can serve as emotional outlets.

Therapeutic Journaling:

Maintain a journal to capture your thoughts and feelings. This serves as a private space for self-reflection and emotional processing.

Mindful Eating Practices:

Practice mindful eating by savoring each bite and paying attention to the flavors and textures of your food. This brings awareness to the present moment and enhances the enjoyment of meals.

Evening Relaxation Rituals:

Establish calming rituals before bedtime. This could include a warm bath, gentle stretching, or listening to soothing music. Creating a tranquil evening routine promotes restful sleep.

Regular Exercise Routine:

Incorporate regular exercise into your routine. Whether it's a workout at the gym, a home exercise routine, or a dance class, physical activity is a powerful tool for enhancing mood and reducing stress.

Social Connection Time:

Schedule regular time for social connections. This could be a virtual coffee date, a phone call with a friend, or participating in group activities that bring a sense of community.

Real-Life Story: Empowering Through Self-Care

Meet Emily, a resilient individual navigating a challenging relationship with a narcissistic partner. As the emotional turbulence in her relationship intensified, Emily recognized the critical need for self-care to safeguard her mental and emotional well-being.

Implementing a morning mindfulness routine became a transformative practice for Emily. Each day, before engaging with the demands of her relationship, she dedicated a few minutes to mindfulness exercises. Deep breathing and guided meditation provided a moment of calm amidst the storm, allowing Emily to center herself and approach the day with increased resilience.

Additionally, Emily embraced therapeutic journaling as a means of processing her emotions. The act of putting pen to paper provided an outlet for her thoughts and feelings, creating a tangible record of her journey. Through journaling, Emily gained insights into patterns of behavior within the relationship and discovered her own strengths and aspirations.

Over time, Emily expanded her self-care practices to include regular nature walks. These outdoor excursions became a sanctuary where she could breathe, reflect, and find solace in the healing embrace of nature. The positive impact of these intentional self-care routines gradually transformed Emily's outlook, fostering a sense of empowerment and resilience.

Factual Insight:

Research published in the Journal of Applied School Psychology emphasizes the positive effects of mindfulness practices on reducing stress and enhancing well-being. Mindfulness has been shown to contribute to improved emotional regulation, increased self-awareness, and overall mental health.

Nurturing the Self for Resilience

Developing self-care routines and practices is an ongoing, intentional journey towards nurturing your inner strength. The story of Emily illustrates the transformative power of these practices in navigating the challenges of a narcissistic relationship. In the next sections, we'll delve into strategies for navigating communication challenges and empowering individuals within the context of such relationships. Stay tuned for insights that will guide you towards resilience and strength amidst the intricacies of narcissism.

Chapter 5: Seeking Professional Support: Navigating Relationships with a Narcissistic Partner

In the intricate dynamics of a relationship with a narcissistic partner, seeking professional support can be a transformative step towards understanding, healing, and reclaiming one's well-being. This chapter explores the vital role of therapy in managing relationships with narcissistic partners and delves into individual and couples counseling options.

Understanding the Role of Therapy:

Validation and Understanding:

Therapy provides a safe and non-judgmental space where individuals can share their experiences and feelings. For those in relationships with narcissistic partners, the validation and understanding offered by a trained therapist can be a crucial source of support.

Insight into Dynamics:

Therapists specializing in narcissistic relationships can offer insights into the dynamics at play. Understanding the underlying factors contributing to the challenges in the relationship is a pivotal step towards informed decision-making.

Emotional Processing:

The emotional toll of a relationship with a narcissistic partner can be overwhelming. Therapy provides a structured environment for emotional processing, allowing individuals to explore and navigate their feelings in a guided and supportive setting.

Building Coping Strategies:

Coping with the challenges posed by a narcissistic partner requires effective strategies. Therapists equip individuals with coping mechanisms tailored to their specific situation, fostering resilience and empowering them to navigate the complexities of the relationship.

Setting and Enforcing Boundaries:

Establishing and enforcing boundaries is a fundamental aspect of managing a relationship with a narcissistic partner. Therapists work with individuals to develop and implement effective boundary-setting strategies, supporting them in maintaining a sense of autonomy.

Decision-Making Support:

Deciding whether to stay in or leave a relationship with a narcissistic partner is a complex choice. Therapists provide a neutral space for individuals to explore their options, offering guidance and support as they make decisions aligned with their well-being.

Individual Counseling

Focus on Personal Growth:

Individual counseling allows individuals to focus on personal growth, self-discovery, and building resilience. Therapists work collaboratively with clients to explore their goals, strengths, and areas for development.

Healing from Emotional Trauma:

For those who have experienced emotional trauma within a narcissistic relationship, individual counseling provides a dedicated space for healing. Therapists employ evidence-based techniques to address the impact of emotional abuse and promote emotional well-being.

Developing Coping Strategies:

Coping with the daily challenges of a narcissistic relationship often requires specific strategies. In individual counseling, clients work with therapists to develop personalized coping mechanisms that align with their unique circumstances and needs.

Couples Counseling

Navigating Communication Challenges:

Couples counseling addresses communication breakdowns within the relationship. Therapists facilitate constructive dialogues, helping partners express their needs and concerns in a more effective and respectful manner.

Building Empathy:

Narcissistic relationships often lack empathy. Couples counseling aims to foster empathy between partners, encouraging a deeper understanding of each other's perspectives and experiences.

Establishing Healthy Dynamics:

Therapists guide couples in restructuring unhealthy dynamics within the relationship. By addressing power imbalances, control issues, and patterns of manipulation, couples can work towards establishing healthier interactions.

Setting Joint Goals:

Collaborative goal-setting is a key aspect of couples counseling. Therapists assist partners in identifying common objectives and aspirations, fostering a shared vision for the relationship's future.

Addressing Codependency:

In narcissistic relationships, codependency is common. Couples counseling provides a space to address codependent dynamics and encourages the development of healthier, more balanced relationship patterns.

Empowering Through Professional Support

Seeking professional support through therapy is a proactive and empowering step for individuals navigating relationships with narcissistic partners. Whether through individual counseling for personal growth and healing or couples counseling to address relationship dynamics, therapists play a crucial role in guiding individuals towards resilience and well-being. In the subsequent sections, we'll further explore strategies for communication and empowerment within the context of narcissistic relationships. Stay tuned for insights that will guide you towards strength and understanding amidst the intricacies of narcissism.

Individual and Couples Counseling Options: Guiding Paths to Healing

In the journey of managing relationships with narcissistic partners, individual and couples counseling emerge as invaluable tools for understanding, healing, and fostering positive change. This chapter explores the options available in individual and couples counseling, offering distinct paths towards personal growth and relationship transformation.

Individual Counseling Options:

Psychoanalytic Therapy:
Focus: Uncovering unconscious patterns and unresolved conflicts.
Benefits: Insight into deep-seated issues, fostering self-awareness.

Cognitive-Behavioral Therapy (CBT):
Focus: Identifying and changing negative thought patterns and behaviors.
Benefits: Developing coping strategies, fostering positive behavioral changes.

Dialectical Behavior Therapy (DBT):
Focus: Emotion regulation, interpersonal effectiveness, distress tolerance.
Benefits: Enhanced emotional resilience, improved interpersonal skills.

Narrative Therapy:
Focus: Restructuring one's life narrative and reframing experiences.
Benefits: Empowerment through the creation of a more positive life story.

Humanistic/Person-Centered Therapy:
Focus: Nurturing personal growth and self-actualization.
Benefits: Fostering self-discovery, enhancing self-esteem.

Trauma-Focused Therapy:
Focus: Addressing the impact of emotional trauma.
Benefits: Healing from traumatic experiences, promoting emotional well-being.

Couples Counseling Options:

Emotionally Focused Therapy (EFT):
Focus: Identifying and reshaping emotional responses in relationships.
Benefits: Improved emotional connection, enhanced communication.

Gottman Method Couples Therapy:
Focus: Building relationship skills and addressing conflict.
Benefits: Strengthening emotional bonds, improving conflict resolution.

Imago Relationship Therapy:
Focus: Understanding and resolving unconscious relationship patterns.
Benefits: Enhanced communication, deeper understanding of partner.

Solution-Focused Brief Therapy (SFBT):
Focus: Identifying and working towards solutions rather than problems.
Benefits: Goal-oriented, practical strategies for positive change.

Integrative Behavioral Couples Therapy (IBCT):
Focus: Balancing acceptance and change in relationships.
Benefits: Improved communication, enhanced emotional intimacy.

Narrative Couples Therapy:
Focus: Exploring and rewriting the narrative of the relationship.
Benefits: Creating a more positive and collaborative relationship story.

Tailoring Therapy Choices:

Assessment:
Conduct an initial assessment to determine individual or couples needs.
Identify specific issues within the relationship dynamic or individual struggles.

Therapist Specialization:
Choose therapists with expertise in narcissistic relationships or related areas.
Seek professionals who align with the chosen therapeutic approach.

Open Communication:
Discuss expectations and goals openly with the therapist.
Establish clear communication channels for feedback and concerns.

Flexibility in Approach:
Be open to adjusting therapy approaches based on progress and feedback.
Flexibility enhances the effectiveness of therapy in addressing unique needs.

Empowering Through Counseling

Individual and couples counseling offer distinctive paths towards healing, understanding, and transformation in relationships with narcissistic partners. The tailored approaches of various therapeutic modalities empower individuals and couples to navigate challenges, build resilience, and foster positive change. In the subsequent sections, we'll delve into communication strategies and empowerment tools within the context of narcissistic relationships.

Chapter 6: Communication Strategies: Navigating the Narcissistic Dynamic

In the intricate dance of a relationship with a narcissistic partner, effective communication becomes a vital tool for understanding, connection, and asserting one's needs. This chapter explores specific examples of communication strategies tailored to navigate the complexities of a narcissistic relationship.

Understanding the Narcissistic Dynamic:

Recognizing narcissistic traits in your partner is the first step to developing effective communication strategies. For instance, if your partner consistently dismisses your feelings or redirects conversations to focus on themselves, you may be dealing with narcissistic behavior. Understanding this dynamic allows you to approach communication with a thoughtful and strategic mindset.

Cultivating emotional awareness is equally essential. Consider a situation where your partner criticizes your choices. Instead of reacting defensively, emotional awareness enables you to recognize your feelings, allowing for a more intentional and measured response.

Communication Strategies:

Stay Calm and Collected:
In the face of criticism or manipulation, maintaining a calm demeanor is crucial. For instance, if your partner attempts to provoke a reaction, responding with composure instead of escalating the situation can defuse tension.

Use Clear and Direct Language:
Imagine your partner consistently undermines your opinions. Using clear and direct language, you might say, "I value my opinions, and it's important for us to respect each other's views."

Establish Boundaries Firmly:
Setting boundaries requires assertiveness. If your partner tends to invade your personal space, a firm but respectful boundary might be, "I need my personal space, and it's important for you to respect that."

Focus on "I" Statements:
When expressing your feelings, using "I" statements can be powerful. For instance, instead of saying, "You never listen," you might say, "I feel unheard when my opinions are dismissed."

Avoid Defensiveness:
Imagine your partner accuses you of being overly sensitive. Instead of becoming defensive, you might respond with, "I understand you have a different perspective, but my feelings are valid, and it's important to address them."

Validate Without Conceding:
If your partner criticizes your choices, you can acknowledge their viewpoint without conceding. For example, "I see that you have concerns, but I also need you to understand why I made this decision."

Stay Goal-Oriented:
In a heated discussion, focusing on specific goals is effective. For example, if a conversation tends to veer off course, you might say, "Let's stay focused on finding a solution to this particular issue."

Pick Your Battles:
Recognizing when to engage is key. If your partner provokes conflict over trivial matters, choosing not to engage in every battle can preserve your emotional well-being.

Practice Active Listening:
Active listening is crucial for empathetic communication. For instance, when your partner expresses frustration, actively listening and acknowledging their feelings can de-escalate tension.

Offer Positive Reinforcement:
Reinforce positive behaviors with encouragement. If your partner shows understanding, expressing appreciation can encourage more constructive communication patterns.

Navigating Conflict and Assertive Expression

Preparation is Key:
Before addressing a concern, clarifying your thoughts is vital. For instance, if your partner consistently undermines your decisions, preparing a clear expression of your feelings and needs can enhance assertiveness.

Use "I" Statements Effectively:
Applying "I" statements assertively is essential. Instead of saying, "You always dismiss my ideas," you might assertively express, "I feel dismissed when my ideas are consistently overlooked."

Express Consequences Clearly:
When setting boundaries, communicating consequences is crucial. For example, "If my boundaries continue to be violated, I'll need to reassess the dynamics of our relationship."

Implement the 24-Hour Rule:
Intense situations often benefit from a cooling-off period. If faced with a highly emotional discussion, implementing the 24-hour rule allows time for reflection and a more measured response.

Seek Compromise, Not Control:
Instead of seeking control, aim for compromise. Finding common ground that respects both perspectives can transform conflict into collaboration.

Navigating Conflict and Assertive Expression: A Balancing Act

In the complex terrain of a relationship with a narcissistic partner, navigating conflicts and expressing needs assertively requires finesse and strategic communication. Picture a scenario where your partner dismisses your concerns, a common behavior in narcissistic dynamics. In such situations, assertive expression becomes a crucial tool for maintaining your boundaries and fostering understanding.

When conflicts arise, consider the implementation of the 24-hour rule, allowing both parties a space for reflection before addressing the issue. This strategic pause prevents impulsive reactions and provides an opportunity for a more thoughtful and constructive conversation. Imagine your partner consistently undermines your decisions. As you prepare to address this concern, clarity in your thoughts and a firm commitment to expressing your needs assertively become paramount.

Assertive communication involves using "I" statements effectively to convey your feelings without accusatory undertones. For instance, you might say, "I feel disregarded when my decisions are consistently dismissed, and it's important for me to be heard and respected." This approach shifts the focus from blame to personal experience, fostering a more open and less confrontational dialogue.

Expressing consequences clearly is another facet of assertive communication. If your partner continually crosses established boundaries, clearly articulating the consequences reinforces accountability. For example, "If my boundaries are consistently violated, I'll need to reassess the dynamics of our relationship to ensure my well-being."

Navigating conflict also involves seeking compromise rather than control. In a scenario where your partner insists on having their way, finding common ground becomes essential. Instead of framing the discussion as a power struggle, shift the focus to collaborative problem-solving, fostering a more cooperative and understanding environment.

The balancing act of assertive expression in the face of narcissistic dynamics requires ongoing self-awareness, emotional intelligence, and a commitment to maintaining healthy boundaries. By integrating these strategies, you can navigate conflicts with intention, express your needs assertively, and foster a more balanced and empowered relationship dynamic.

Expressing consequences clearly is another facet of assertive communication. If your partner continually crosses established boundaries, clearly articulating the consequences reinforces accountability. For example, "If my boundaries are consistently violated, I'll need to reassess the dynamics of our relationship to ensure my well-being."

Navigating conflict also involves seeking compromise rather than control. In a scenario where your partner insists on having their way, finding common ground becomes essential. Instead of framing the discussion as a power struggle, shift the focus to collaborative problem-solving, fostering a more and understanding environment.

The balancing act of assertive expression in the face of narcissistic dynamics requires ongoing self-awareness, emotional intelligence, and a commitment to maintaining healthy boundaries. By integrating these strategies, you can navigate conflicts with intention, express your needs assertively, and foster a more balanced and empowered relationship dynamic.

Chapter 7: Empowerment and Independence: Nurturing Personal Growth

In the intricate landscape of a relationship with a narcissistic partner, the pursuit of personal growth and independence emerges as a transformative journey, a pathway to reclaiming agency and fortifying one's sense of self. Picture a scenario where individual aspirations are often eclipsed by the dominance of a narcissistic dynamic; in such circumstances, the quest for empowerment becomes paramount.

Cultivating personal growth within the context of a narcissistic relationship involves a deliberate commitment to self-discovery and continuous development. This journey begins with the acknowledgment of one's intrinsic worth and the recognition that personal aspirations are not only valid but essential for a fulfilling life. Whether through educational pursuits, career advancement, or the exploration of personal interests and hobbies, the pursuit of individual goals becomes a crucial means of fostering self-identity.

Setting and pursuing personal goals, independent of the relationship, provides a sense of purpose and accomplishment. Engaging in activities that fuel passion and curiosity contributes not only to personal fulfillment but also serves as a vehicle for self-discovery. This intentional pursuit of personal growth creates a narrative beyond the confines of the narcissistic dynamic, allowing individuals to nurture a sense of autonomy and agency over their lives.

Financial independence is a cornerstone of empowerment within a relationship marked by narcissistic traits. Establishing financial autonomy entails creating a foundation of economic self-reliance, reducing dependency on the partner's financial control. This could involve managing personal finances, exploring career opportunities, or seeking financial advice to ensure a stable and secure future. Financial independence not only provides a tangible means of empowerment but also acts as a protective measure against potential manipulation and control.

Emotional resilience becomes a vital aspect of fostering independence within the confines of a narcissistic relationship. The emotional rollercoaster often associated with such dynamics necessitates the development of coping mechanisms and self-care practices. This involves setting and enforcing clear emotional boundaries, prioritizing mental well-being, and seeking therapeutic support when needed. By nurturing emotional resilience, individuals can navigate the challenges of the relationship while safeguarding their mental and emotional health.

Building a robust support network is an instrumental component of fostering independence. The isolation often perpetuated by narcissistic dynamics can be mitigated through connections with friends, family, or support groups. These external relationships offer a source of validation, understanding, and encouragement, counteracting the potential isolation imposed by the narcissistic partner. Cultivating these connections serves as a reminder of one's inherent worth and provides a crucial anchor in the journey towards independence.

The pursuit of personal growth and independence requires a mindset shift that prioritizes self-compassion and self-advocacy. This involves challenging ingrained beliefs that may have been shaped by the narcissistic dynamic, reaffirming one's worth, and embracing the agency to shape one's own narrative. The journey towards empowerment is a process of reclaiming personal autonomy and recognizing the right to pursue individual happiness and fulfillment.

Within the web of a relationship marked by narcissistic traits, preserving a sense of self becomes a nuanced journey, requiring intentional strategies and a steadfast commitment to personal identity. In the relentless ebb and flow of narcissistic dynamics, individuals often find their autonomy compromised, their aspirations overshadowed. Yet, amidst these challenges, specific strategies can serve as beacons of self-preservation, allowing individuals to navigate the complexities while fostering personal growth.

One pivotal strategy is the cultivation and affirmation of personal boundaries. Establishing clear and non-negotiable boundaries is essential for delineating the contours of selfhood within the relationship. Whether it involves delineating personal space, asserting emotional limits, or safeguarding time for individual pursuits, boundaries serve as a protective framework, defining the space where one's identity can thrive. The communication of these boundaries, done assertively yet respectfully, becomes a crucial aspect of preserving individuality.

An integral component of maintaining a sense of self involves fostering self-awareness. In the labyrinth of narcissistic dynamics, it is easy to lose sight of one's own needs, desires, and emotional well-being. Cultivating self-awareness involves regular reflection on personal values, aspirations, and emotions. This introspective practice not only fortifies one's connection to self but also enables a more informed navigation of the relationship dynamics. Journaling, mindfulness, and self-reflection exercises can be invaluable tools in this ongoing process.

The pursuit of personal interests and passions stands as a beacon of self-preservation. Actively engaging in activities that bring joy, fulfillment, and a sense of purpose contributes significantly to maintaining individual identity. Whether it's a creative pursuit, a hobby, or involvement in a community, these endeavors act as anchors, grounding individuals in their unique strengths and aspirations.

This intentional pursuit of personal interests fosters a narrative beyond the immediate relational context, allowing for a multifaceted sense of self to flourish.

Cultivating emotional resilience emerges as a vital strategy in navigating the emotional turbulence inherent in narcissistic relationships. This involves developing coping mechanisms to manage the emotional impact of manipulation, criticism, or gaslighting. Seeking support through therapy or support groups provides a valuable outlet for processing emotions and gaining tools to navigate the intricacies of the relationship. Emotional resilience serves as a shield, preserving one's mental well-being amidst the storm of narcissistic dynamics.

The intentional creation of a support network outside the confines of the narcissistic relationship is a powerful strategy for maintaining a sense of self. Establishing connections with friends, family, or support groups provides a lifeline of understanding, validation, and encouragement. These external relationships not only offer a source of emotional support but also counteract the potential isolation imposed by the narcissistic partner. Building a robust support network becomes a cornerstone of preserving one's sense of worth and individuality.

Developing and pursuing personal goals stands as a transformative strategy for maintaining a sense of self. Whether professional, educational, or personal, setting and achieving goals contribute to a sense of accomplishment and agency.

This intentional pursuit of personal growth extends beyond the relational dynamics, reinforcing the understanding that individual aspirations are not only valid but crucial for a fulfilling life. The achievement of personal goals becomes a testament to one's capabilities and a reminder of the agency to shape one's own narrative.

Maintaining open and honest communication with the narcissistic partner, when possible, is a strategic yet challenging approach. This involves expressing one's needs, desires, and boundaries assertively while navigating potential resistance or manipulation. Clear communication not only reinforces personal boundaries but also fosters a more transparent relational dynamic. While it may not always be met with receptivity, honest communication becomes a tool for asserting individuality within the relationship.

The integration of these multifaceted strategies forms a comprehensive approach to maintaining a sense of self within the intricate dynamics of a narcissistic relationship. It is a journey marked by resilience, self-compassion, and a steadfast commitment to personal growth. As individuals navigate these strategies, they empower themselves to not only endure the challenges but also thrive in the pursuit of autonomy and fulfillment. In the subsequent chapters, we will delve into additional insights and tools for empowerment within the context of narcissistic relationships, guiding individuals towards strength and understanding amidst the intricacies of these dynamics.

Chapter 8: Cultivating Healthy Relationships Outside the Partnership: The Crucial Role of a Support Network

In the challenging terrain of a relationship marked by narcissistic dynamics, the importance of cultivating healthy relationships outside the partnership cannot be overstated. The isolation perpetuated within such relationships underscores the need for a robust support network, a lifeline that offers understanding, validation, and a sense of belonging. Within the intricate dance of narcissistic dynamics, building and maintaining connections with friends and family emerges as not just a choice but a vital strategy for preserving mental well-being, fostering resilience, and affirming one's identity.

A fundamental aspect of cultivating a support network lies in recognizing the inherent limitations of relying solely on the narcissistic partner for emotional sustenance. The unpredictable and often manipulative nature of such relationships can leave individuals emotionally drained and isolated. In this context, friends and family become invaluable pillars, providing a stable foundation of emotional support that counters the potential emotional turbulence within the primary partnership.

Building and maintaining relationships with friends and family act as a safeguard against the insidious effects of gaslighting and manipulation often present in narcissistic dynamics.

The validation and empathy offered by an external support network serve as a reality check, affirming the individual's experiences and feelings. This external perspective becomes instrumental in countering the distortions of reality that may be imposed within the narcissistic relationship, offering clarity and a grounding force.

The role of friends in cultivating a healthy support network cannot be understated. Genuine friendships provide a space for authenticity, where individuals can express themselves without fear of judgment or manipulation. Friends become a source of encouragement, laughter, and shared experiences, creating a counterbalance to the emotional intensity within the narcissistic partnership. Cultivating deep, meaningful friendships fosters a sense of belonging and strengthens the individual's resilience.

Family, as a component of the support network, carries a unique significance. While family dynamics can be complex, maintaining connections with supportive family members offers a sense of continuity, history, and shared identity. Family can serve as a source of unconditional love and understanding, contributing to a feeling of rootedness that becomes especially crucial in navigating the challenges of a narcissistic relationship.

Strategically building relationships outside the partnership involves intentional effort. Actively engaging in social activities, joining clubs or groups aligned with personal interests, and attending social gatherings create opportunities for forging new connections. These external relationships not only provide emotional support but also diversify the individual's social interactions, offering a broader perspective on life beyond the confines of the narcissistic dynamic.

The reciprocation of care within a support network is a cornerstone of its effectiveness. Being there for friends and family members, offering support and empathy in return, fosters a sense of mutual reliance. This reciprocity strengthens the bonds within the support network, creating a dynamic where individuals feel valued and understood. The communal nature of a support network becomes a source of collective resilience, where each member contributes to the well-being of the whole.

Moreover, the encouragement to seek professional help or therapy within a support network can be a crucial intervention. Friends and family members, acting as advocates for mental well-being, can play a pivotal role in encouraging individuals to prioritize their mental health. The external perspective of a therapist can complement the support network, offering specialized guidance and tools for navigating the complexities of a narcissistic relationship.

In essence, the cultivation of healthy relationships outside the partnership is a deliberate and transformative strategy for individuals navigating narcissistic dynamics. The support network acts as a counterforce against isolation, manipulation, and emotional turmoil, offering a sanctuary of understanding and validation. As we delve into the subsequent chapters, we will explore additional insights and tools for empowerment within the context of narcissistic relationships, guiding individuals towards strength and understanding amidst the intricacies of these dynamics.

Building and Maintaining Relationships with Friends and Family: A Sanctuary Beyond Narcissistic Dynamics

In the intricate dance of a relationship marked by narcissistic traits, the intentional building and maintenance of connections with friends and family emerge as an essential strategy for preserving mental well-being, fostering resilience, and affirming one's identity. This deliberate cultivation of a support network acts as a counterbalance to the isolation and emotional turbulence often perpetuated within the narcissistic partnership. In navigating the complexities of these dynamics, the significance of healthy relationships outside the primary partnership cannot be overstated.

Recognizing the Limitations of Sole Reliance:
At the core of building relationships outside the partnership lies the recognition of the inherent limitations of relying solely on the narcissistic partner for emotional sustenance.

IThe unpredictable nature and potential manipulations within such relationships can lead to emotional exhaustion and isolation. Friends and family, then, become invaluable allies, providing stability, empathy, and a sense of belonging that counteracts the emotional tumult within the primary relationship.

A Safeguard Against Gaslighting and Manipulation:
Friends and family play a crucial role as a safeguard against the insidious effects of gaslighting and manipulation often present in narcissistic dynamics. The validation and understanding offered by an external support network act as a reality check, affirming an individual's experiences and feelings. This external perspective becomes instrumental in countering distortions of reality, offering clarity and grounding in moments of doubt or confusion.

The Role of Friends in Emotional Sustenance:
Genuine friendships create a space for authenticity, where individuals can express themselves without fear of judgment or manipulation. Friends become a source of encouragement, laughter, and shared experiences, serving as a counterbalance to the emotional intensity within the narcissistic partnership. Cultivating deep, meaningful friendships fosters a sense of belonging and strengthens the individual's emotional resilience.

Family Dynamics and Unconditional Support:
While family dynamics can be complex, maintaining connections with supportive family members offers a sense of continuity, history, and shared identity. Family becomes a source of unconditional love and understanding, contributing to a feeling of rootedness that becomes especially crucial in navigating the challenges of a narcissistic relationship. Strengthening bonds with family members who provide genuine support creates a familial safety net.

Strategic Efforts in Building External Connections:
Strategically building relationships outside the partnership involves intentional efforts to expand one's social circle. Actively engaging in social activities, joining clubs or groups aligned with personal interests, and attending social gatherings create opportunities for forging new connections. These external relationships not only provide emotional support but also diversify the individual's social interactions, offering a broader perspective on life beyond the confines of the narcissistic dynamic.

Reciprocation and Mutual Reliance:
The reciprocation of care within a support network is a cornerstone of its effectiveness. Being there for friends and family members, offering support and empathy in return, fosters a sense of mutual reliance. This reciprocity strengthens the bonds within the support network, creating a dynamic where individuals feel valued and understood. The communal nature of a support network becomes a source of collective resilience, where each member contributes to the well-being of the whole.

Encouraging Professional Help Within the Network:
Friends and family members can also play a crucial role in encouraging individuals to seek professional help or therapy. Acting as advocates for mental well-being, they contribute to the normalization of seeking help when navigating the challenges of a narcissistic relationship. The external perspective of a therapist can complement the support network, offering specialized guidance and tools for individuals dealing with the complexities of their situation.

The intentional building and maintenance of relationships with friends and family serve as a sanctuary beyond the confines of narcissistic dynamics. This support network becomes a lifeline, offering understanding, validation, and a sense of belonging. As individuals nurture these external connections, they empower themselves to not only endure the challenges but also thrive in the pursuit of autonomy and fulfillment. In the upcoming chapters, we will continue to explore additional insights and tools for empowerment within the context of narcissistic relationships, guiding individuals towards strength and understanding amidst the intricacies of these dynamics.

Chapter 9: Assessing Long-Term Viability: Navigating the Waters of Relationship Health

In the labyrinth of a relationship marked by narcissistic dynamics, the crucial juncture of assessing long-term viability becomes a reflective process, demanding introspection and a clear-eyed evaluation of the partnership's overall health and sustainability. This assessment is a pivotal step, a moment where individuals weigh the costs and benefits, acknowledging the intricacies and challenges inherent in a relationship shaped by narcissistic traits.

As individuals stand at this crossroads, the journey of self-reflection takes center stage. It involves a profound exploration of personal values, aspirations, and well-being within the context of the relationship. Questions about emotional fulfillment, personal growth, and the alignment of values become focal points. Self-reflection becomes a compass, guiding individuals through the complex terrain of their emotions and providing clarity about the path ahead.

Understanding the Dynamics of Narcissistic Traits:
A crucial component of assessing long-term viability is a nuanced understanding of narcissistic traits and their impact on the relationship. Individuals delve into the patterns of manipulation, gaslighting, and emotional turbulence characteristic of such dynamics. This understanding becomes a tool for distinguishing between the challenges inherent in any relationship and those specifically tied to narcissistic behavior. Awareness lays the foundation for informed decision-making.

Weighing Emotional Costs and Benefits:
The emotional toll of navigating a relationship with narcissistic dynamics is a central consideration in the assessment process. Individuals weigh the emotional costs, acknowledging the potential impact on mental well-being, self-esteem, and overall happiness. Simultaneously, they reflect on any emotional benefits or growth that may have occurred within the relationship. This internal balancing act serves as a pivotal gauge for determining the relationship's impact on one's overall life satisfaction.

Exploring Patterns of Manipulation and Gaslighting:
In the assessment of long-term viability, exploration of patterns of manipulation and gaslighting becomes imperative. Individuals scrutinize instances where their reality may have been distorted, and their perceptions undermined. Recognizing these patterns sheds light on the power dynamics within the relationship, empowering individuals to set boundaries and navigate potential manipulation with a clearer understanding.

Considering Individual and Shared Growth:
The evaluation extends beyond the individual to encompass the potential for both personal and shared growth within the relationship. Individuals contemplate whether the partnership has facilitated their personal development or if it has acted as a hindrance. Assessing shared growth involves an examination of communication dynamics, mutual support, and the fostering of each other's aspirations. This comprehensive exploration informs the narrative of the relationship's impact on individual and collective trajectories.

Acknowledging the Impact on Well-being:
Central to the assessment is the acknowledgment of the relationship's impact on overall well-being. Individuals gauge the influence of the partnership on their mental, emotional, and physical health. The presence or absence of a sense of safety and security within the relationship becomes a crucial factor. Honest reflection on whether the partnership contributes positively or poses a risk to well-being forms the cornerstone of the assessment process.

The Role of External Perspectives:
External perspectives from friends, family, or therapeutic support play a vital role in the assessment of long-term viability. Seeking input from those outside the relationship provides valuable insights, offering perspectives unclouded by the emotional intricacies within the partnership. Friends and family become sounding boards, and therapists offer professional guidance, contributing to a more holistic understanding of the relationship's dynamics.

Navigating the Decision-Making Process:
As individuals navigate the decision-making process, they grapple with the potential outcomes and choices that lie ahead. The assessment of long-term viability is a precursor to exploring potential paths, whether it involves committing to intentional changes within the relationship, seeking external support, or contemplating the prospect of separation. This decision-making process is nuanced, individualized, and deeply personal.

Assessing the long-term viability of a relationship marked by narcissistic dynamics is a multidimensional endeavor. It involves a careful weighing of emotional costs and benefits, an exploration of growth potential, and an acknowledgment of the relationship's impact on overall well-being. As individuals embark on this reflective journey, they equip themselves with the insights needed to make informed decisions about the future.

Exploring Potential Outcomes and Decisions: Navigating the Crossroads of Relationship Choices

In the profound journey of assessing the long-term viability of a relationship marked by narcissistic dynamics, the exploration of potential outcomes and decisions becomes a crucial phase, demanding careful consideration and introspection. Individuals find themselves at a crossroads, faced with a myriad of choices that hold the power to shape their future. As they navigate this intricate terrain, the exploration of potential paths becomes a deeply personal and reflective process.

One potential outcome involves a commitment to intentional changes within the relationship. This choice acknowledges the complexities of narcissistic dynamics but underscores the possibility of transformation through concerted effort. It involves setting clear boundaries, fostering open communication, and seeking therapeutic support to address underlying issues. The commitment to change is a joint effort, requiring both partners to engage in self-reflection and actively work towards creating a healthier relational dynamic.

Seeking External Support and Therapeutic Intervention:
Another avenue individuals may explore is seeking external support and therapeutic intervention. This decision recognizes the unique challenges posed by narcissistic dynamics and embraces the idea that professional guidance can offer valuable insights. Couples therapy, individual counseling, or support groups become vehicles for navigating the complexities of the relationship. Therapeutic intervention provides a structured space for addressing communication breakdowns, building empathy, and fostering healthier relational patterns.

Contemplating the Prospect of Separation:
Contemplating the prospect of separation is a profound choice that individuals may consider in the face of insurmountable challenges within the relationship. This decision acknowledges the emotional toll of narcissistic dynamics and prioritizes individual well-being. Separation becomes a means of reclaiming autonomy, establishing healthier boundaries, and creating space for personal growth. It is a decision rooted in self-preservation and the acknowledgment that some relationships may not be conducive to long-term happiness and fulfillment.

Navigating the Complexity of Co-Parenting:
For individuals with children, the exploration of potential outcomes extends to navigating the complexity of co-parenting in the event of separation. This choice involves a commitment to prioritizing the well-being of the children while disentangling from a challenging relationship.

Co-parenting arrangements require clear communication, mutual respect, and a focus on providing stability for the children despite the changes in the familial structure. Navigating this path involves a dedication to fostering a healthy co-parenting dynamic for the benefit of the children involved.

Establishing Independence and Self-Discovery:
In cases where separation is not an immediate option, individuals may explore the path of establishing independence and self-discovery within the existing relationship. This choice involves a commitment to personal growth, pursuing individual interests, and fortifying a sense of self within the context of the partnership. It requires setting and maintaining firm boundaries, actively engaging in self-care practices, and fostering emotional resilience. Establishing independence becomes a proactive choice to reclaim agency and autonomy within the relationship.

Creating a Safety Plan for Emotional Well-Being:
For those who find themselves in relationships marked by more severe forms of narcissistic abuse, the exploration of potential outcomes may include creating a safety plan for emotional well-being. This choice involves strategic measures to protect oneself from emotional harm, including seeking support from friends and family, documenting instances of abuse, and considering legal avenues if necessary. The focus is on prioritizing one's safety and mental health in the face of challenging circumstances.

Deciding on a Timetable for Change:
As individuals explore potential outcomes, they may also contemplate the decision of establishing a timetable for change within the relationship. This choice involves setting clear milestones and expectations for progress. It acknowledges that change within a relationship, especially one marked by narcissistic dynamics, may take time. Establishing a timetable becomes a proactive approach to assess the effectiveness of interventions and evaluate the feasibility of long-term change.

Empowering Oneself Through Informed Decision-Making:
In navigating the exploration of potential outcomes and decisions, the overarching goal is to empower oneself through informed decision-making. This empowerment stems from a deep understanding of the unique dynamics at play, a recognition of personal needs and boundaries, and a commitment to prioritizing one's well-being. Each individual's journey is unique, and the chosen path reflects a deeply personal response to the complexities of a relationship marked by narcissistic traits.

Exploring potential outcomes and decisions within the context of a relationship with narcissistic dynamics is a profound and multifaceted process. It requires a blend of self-reflection, courage, and a commitment to prioritizing one's well-being. As individuals navigate these choices, they embark on a transformative journey towards self-discovery, growth, and the pursuit of a future aligned with their values and aspirations.

Conclusion: Navigating the Complexities of a Relationship with a Narcissistic Partner

In concluding our exploration of the intricacies involved in navigating a relationship with a narcissistic partner, it becomes imperative to recap key strategies that serve as guiding principles in this challenging journey. These strategies are not prescriptive solutions but rather nuanced approaches aimed at fostering resilience, reclaiming autonomy, and prioritizing well-being within the context of narcissistic dynamics.

Setting and Communicating Clear Boundaries:
A foundational strategy is the establishment and communication of clear boundaries. Boundaries serve as protective shields, delineating personal space, emotional limits, and expectations within the relationship. Communicating these boundaries assertively, though challenging, is crucial for creating a framework that safeguards individual well-being.

Cultivating Emotional Resilience:
Cultivating emotional resilience emerges as a vital strategy in navigating the emotional rollercoaster inherent in narcissistic relationships. This involves developing coping mechanisms, practicing self-care, and seeking therapeutic support to fortify mental and emotional well-being. Emotional resilience becomes a shield against the potential impact of manipulation and gaslighting.

Fostering Personal Growth and Independence:
Prioritizing personal growth and independence is a transformative strategy that involves pursuing individual goals, interests, and passions outside the confines of the relationship. This intentional cultivation of self-identity serves as a counterbalance to the potential erosion of autonomy within the narcissistic dynamic. It becomes a proactive choice to reclaim agency and pursue a fulfilling life beyond the partnership.

Building and Maintaining a Support Network:
The cultivation of healthy relationships outside the partnership forms a crucial pillar in navigating the complexities of narcissistic dynamics. Building and maintaining connections with friends and family provide a lifeline of understanding, validation, and support. This external network becomes a sanctuary, offering perspectives unclouded by the emotional intricacies within the relationship.

Strategic Communication and Honesty:
Effective communication within the relationship, marked by strategic honesty, becomes a cornerstone for navigating narcissistic dynamics. This involves expressing needs, desires, and boundaries assertively while navigating potential resistance or manipulation. Clear communication fosters transparency, contributing to a more informed relational dynamic.

Exploring Personal Interests and Hobbies:
The intentional exploration of personal interests and hobbies becomes a proactive strategy for preserving individuality within the relationship. Engaging in activities that bring joy and fulfillment contributes to a multifaceted sense of self. This pursuit serves as an anchor, grounding individuals in their unique strengths and aspirations.

Assessing Long-Term Viability:
As individuals reach a critical juncture in their journey, the assessment of the long-term viability of the relationship becomes a pivotal strategy. This involves a reflective process, considering emotional costs and benefits, understanding the impact on well-being, and exploring patterns of manipulation. The assessment serves as a compass for informed decision-making about the future.

Exploring Potential Outcomes and Decisions:
The exploration of potential outcomes and decisions further extends the journey of empowerment. Whether committing to intentional changes, seeking external support, contemplating separation, or establishing a timetable for change, individuals engage in a deeply personal and reflective process. This exploration involves a careful weighing of options, acknowledging personal boundaries, and navigating the complexities of relational choices.

These strategies collectively form a toolkit for individuals navigating relationships marked by narcissistic traits. It's essential to recognize that every journey is unique, and the application of these strategies may vary based on individual circumstances. Navigating a relationship with a narcissistic partner requires ongoing self-reflection, adaptability, and a commitment to prioritizing one's well-being. As we conclude this exploration, we will continue to offer encouragement for personal growth and well-being, recognizing that the journey towards empowerment is an ongoing process of self-discovery and resilience.

Encouragement for Personal Growth and Well-being: Thriving Beyond Narcissistic Dynamics

As we conclude this exploration, it is paramount to extend heartfelt encouragement for personal growth and well-being to those navigating the intricate terrain of relationships marked by narcissistic dynamics. The journey embarked upon is undeniably challenging, fraught with emotional complexities and moments of self-discovery. In the face of these challenges, however, there exists an immense potential for transformative growth, resilience, and the reclamation of one's narrative.

Embrace the Power of Self-Discovery:
The first step towards personal growth involves embracing the power of self-discovery. This journey is an opportunity to delve deep into the intricacies of one's values, aspirations, and authentic self. Uncover the layers that may have been overshadowed by the dynamics of the relationship. Self-discovery is not a destination but a continuous process, allowing for the unfolding of one's true essence over time.

Nurture Your Inner Resilience:
Resilience is the companion that walks alongside individuals facing the challenges posed by narcissistic dynamics. Cultivate and nurture your inner resilience, acknowledging that every trial is an opportunity for growth. Recognize the strength that resides within, allowing you to weather storms and emerge stronger. Resilience becomes a guiding force, propelling you forward even in the face of adversity.

Prioritize Self-Care as a Non-Negotiable:
Amidst the demands of navigating a relationship marked by narcissistic traits, prioritize self-care as a non-negotiable aspect of your routine. This involves intentional practices that nurture your mental, emotional, and physical well-being. Whether it's dedicating time to activities that bring joy, seeking therapeutic support, or simply resting when needed, self-care becomes a powerful tool for rejuvenation.

Celebrate Milestones, No Matter How Small:
In the journey towards personal growth, celebrate milestones, no matter how small they may seem. Each step forward, each moment of self-assertion, and every instance of setting boundaries is a victory worthy of acknowledgment. These milestones collectively contribute to the narrative of your resilience and progress. Celebrate your journey with compassion and pride.

Forge Connections Beyond the Relationship:
As you continue to navigate the complexities of the relationship, forge connections beyond its confines. Cultivate relationships with friends, family, and support networks that offer understanding, validation, and unconditional support. These connections act as pillars of strength, providing a sense of belonging and a reminder that you are not alone in your journey.

Embrace Change as a Catalyst for Growth:
Change, though often challenging, can be a catalyst for profound growth. Embrace the shifts and transformations that may unfold as you navigate the path ahead. Recognize that change is not a sign of weakness but an affirmation of your ability to adapt and evolve. It is through change that new possibilities for personal growth emerge.

Affirm Your Worth and Individuality:
In the face of narcissistic dynamics, affirm your worth and individuality as non-negotiable aspects of your identity. Recognize that your value extends beyond the constraints of the relationship. Affirmation becomes an act of self-love, reinforcing the understanding that you deserve respect, understanding, and the freedom to express your authentic self.

Cultivate a Vision for Your Future:
As you navigate the complexities of the present, cultivate a vision for your future. Envision the life you aspire to lead, one that aligns with your values, aspirations, and well-being. This vision serves as a guiding light, motivating you to take intentional steps towards the fulfillment of your dreams, independent of the challenges you currently face.

Acknowledge Your Progress with Compassion:
In moments of reflection, acknowledge your progress with compassion. Recognize that personal growth is a journey marked by both triumphs and setbacks. Approach yourself with the same kindness you would extend to a friend, understanding that growth is a continuous process that unfolds at its own pace.

Concluding Thoughts: A Journey of Empowerment:
As we bring this exploration to a close, remember that your journey is one of empowerment and resilience. You possess the strength to navigate the complexities of relationships marked by narcissistic dynamics. Your commitment to personal growth and well-being is a testament to your unwavering spirit.

In choosing to prioritize your own flourishing, you embark on a path that transcends the limitations imposed by the challenges you face. Your journey becomes a beacon of inspiration for others who may be navigating similar landscapes. In every step forward, in every act of self-care, and in every pursuit of personal growth, you redefine the narrative of your own strength and resilience.

May your path be filled with self-discovery, may your resilience be unwavering, and may your well-being be the compass that guides you towards a future enriched with fulfillment and authenticity. As you continue your journey, know that you are not alone, and the possibilities for personal growth are boundless. May this chapter of your life be marked by empowerment, self-love, and the unwavering belief in your own strength.

Wishing you courage, compassion, and an abundance of moments that contribute to your personal growth and well-being.

www.ingramcontent.com/pod-product-compliance
Lightning Source LLC
Chambersburg PA
CBHW060957260726
48661CB00005B/1920